P9-DCR-611

JUNIOR
BIOGRAPHIES

Therese M. Shea

CAM
NEWTON
MVP QUARTERBACK

Enslow Publishing

101 W. 23rd Street
Suite 240
New York, NY 10011
USA

enslow.com

draft The process by which players are chosen to enter a sports league.

foundation A group that is formed to do something that helps others.

fumble To fail to catch or hold the ball.

interception The act of catching or receiving a pass made by an opponent.

rookie A player in his or her first year on a team.

rush To move a football forward by running plays.

scholarship Money that is given to a student to help pay for school costs.

scout A person whose job is to find talented athletes for teams.

turnover The act of a team losing possession of a ball through error.

varsity The main team that represents a school.

CONTENTS

Cam Newton

Quarterback Cam Newton is known for his Superman celebration on the field. He acts like the comic book hero. He pretends to rip off his shirt to reveal the famous "S" underneath. People even call Cam "Superman" or "Super Cam."

Cameron Jerrell Newton was born on May 11, 1989, in College Park, Georgia, near Atlanta. He was the second of three boys in the family. Their father, Cecil, encouraged them to play football. He had played in college but didn't make it into the NFL (National Football League). He wanted his

Cam Says:

"I get butterflies before the game, but I wouldn't call that nervous at all. More like excited before Christmas morning."

Cam's family at an awards ceremony, from left to right: his father, Cecil Sr., his mother, Jackie, and brothers Caylin and Cecil Jr.

sons to succeed where he had failed. The boys' parents also made sure they kept up in school and worked to earn money for things they wanted.

HIGH SCHOOL STAR

When the Newton brothers and their friends played football, Cam was faster and more skilled than the older boys. He played both offense and defense before becoming quarterback. Cam made it onto his high school **varsity** team his freshman year. His first start was not pretty—he **fumbled** a pass from his brother and lost the game.

Cam grew in skill and size, though. By his senior year, he was 6 foot 4 inches (193 centimeters) and weighed 230 pounds (104 kilograms). He could run, catch, tackle, and throw 75 yards. He was known for laughing and joking around, but he was very serious on the field.

Cam Newton is 6 feet 5 inches (196 cm) and 245 pounds (111 kg). He has the big body of a linebacker and the speed of a tailback.

G 10 20 30 40 50 40 30 20 10 G

CHAPTER 2
THE QUEST FOR COLLEGE

College scouts took notice of Cam's high school career. He got scholarship offers from many schools. Cam decided to go to the University of Florida. However, the Gators' starting quarterback—Tim Tebow—performed so well that Cam did not see much playing time. Then, Cam was hurt during Florida's 2008 championship season.

Cam finally chose to leave Florida. He did not know if his career was going anywhere or if he should even play football anymore. He took a chance and went to Blinn College, where he had an amazing season. He threw for 2,833 yards and 22 touchdowns. He led the Blinn Buccaneers to the junior college national championship.

Blinn College is a junior college in Texas. Coach Brad Franchione worked with Cam there, teaching him about leadership. The players did not just work hard on the field—they painted the bleachers for their fans!

G 10 20 30 40 50 40 50 20 10

At Blinn, Cam ran for 102 yards in an incredible comeback win in the NJCAA National Football Championship.

Cam heads into the locker room at Auburn University.

THE ROAD TO THE NFL

Once again, many top football programs noticed Cam's strong performance. This time, Cam chose the Auburn Tigers. He had a jaw-dropping 2010 season, with an undefeated 13–0 record. One of the highlights was a comeback win against Alabama. They were behind 24–0, but the Tigers came back to win 28–27, thanks to 3 touchdown passes. Auburn easily won the SEC Championship and the BCS National Championship.

Cam Says:

"Honestly, winning the Heisman Trophy is a dream come true for me. I'm living testimony that anything is possible."

On December 11, 2010, Cam Newton received the Heisman Trophy as the most outstanding college football player. It was time for the NFL.

Cam accepts the Heisman Trophy award in 2010.

CHAPTER 3
A CAROLINA PANTHER

The Carolina Panthers chose Cam Newton as the first overall pick in the 2011 NFL Draft. He won the team's starter slot and right away he made a splash. Against the Arizona Cardinals, Cam threw 422 passing yards and 2 touchdowns. He also ran in a touchdown himself.

Despite this start, the Panthers ended the season 6–10. Cam had struggled with turnovers, but he was great at getting the ball into the end zone. He broke the record for most passing yards by a rookie quarterback with 4,051 and was named AP Offensive Rookie of the Year.

ANOTHER HARD YEAR

Cam's 2012 season was a rockier one. The team ended up 7–9 overall. However, Cam

Cam Says:

"Give up, that's what they want you to do. Stop, that's what they want you to do. You're not the best, that's what they say. Come on, let's be great."

Cam had 14 rushing touchdowns and 21 passing touchdowns in his rookie year for the Carolina Panthers.

improved in some ways, rushing for a career-high 72-yard touchdown in a game versus Atlanta and cutting back on interceptions by the season's end.

In 2013, Cam led the Panthers in a 12–4 season and to the playoffs for the first time. They lost to the San Francisco 49ers in the NFC divisional playoff. Despite being hurt in 2014, Cam and Carolina won the NFC South

Cam was named NEC Offensive Player of the Week after the December 7, 2014, game against New Orleans. He had 309 yards and four touchdowns!

division title once again, only to lose in the divisional playoffs once more.

A SUPER SEASON

In 2015, Newton's winning ways continued. He totaled 35 passing touchdowns, just 10 interceptions, and rushed another 10 touchdowns. He led the Panthers to a remarkable 15–1 record and was named the NFL MVP. This amazing season ended with the Panthers meeting the Denver Broncos in Super Bowl 50.

The game was close, and both the Broncos' quarterback Peyton Manning and

Cam Newton became the first player in NFL history with at least 30 passing touchdowns in a single season.

Cam Newton could not perform his usual heroics against a strong Denver defense in Super Bowl 50.

Cam struggled. The game was called one of the most defensive Super Bowl matchups ever, with each team picking up sacks and forcing turnovers. Cam ended up as the Panthers' leading rusher, but Carolina lost to Denver 24–10.

CHAPTER 4
IMPROVING AND INSPIRING

Cam Newton has plenty of interests off the field—and that includes improving others' lives. He says his parents helped him know what it means to work hard on the field and try to be a good person off it.

The quarterback's Cam Newton **Foundation** was formed to help young people. The group works to help students succeed in school in many ways. It also helps children to stay healthy through sports by fixing up playgrounds and creating sports programs.

Cam Says:

"I am most proud of the fact that I am a recent college graduate. I worked hard at it...and it is an accomplishment that will benefit me long after I'm done playing football."

LOOKING AHEAD

In the opening game of the 2016 season, Cam Newton earned another impressive record. His 44th rushing

Cam enjoys helping children. His foundation helps kids in need get healthy and do better in school.

Fans love Cam Newton's colorful touchdown celebrations and dances.

touchdown of his career was the most of any quarterback in NFL history.

Cam does not think he was born a great athlete. "Greatness is earned," he says. He promises that Super Bowl 50 was not his peak. He plans to earn his Super Bowl ring. Cam continues to find ways to take every part of his game to the next level. This "superman" of football has more in store for fans—both on and off the field.

No quarterback has more seasons with at least 3,000 passing yards and 500 rushing yards than Cam Newton.

1989 Cameron "Cam" Jerrell Newton is born May 11 in College Park, Georgia.

2003 Makes his high school varsity team in his freshman year.

2007 Joins the University of Florida Gators.

2009 Leads Blinn College to win the NJCAA National Football Championship.

2010 Leads Auburn University to win the BCS National Championship and is awarded the Heisman Trophy.

2011 Is chosen by the Carolina Panthers as the first overall pick in the NFL Draft.

2016 Wins the NFL MVP award; Panthers lose to the Denver Broncos in Super Bowl 50.

2016 Claims the record for most rushing touchdowns by an NFL quarterback.

BOOKS

The Charlotte Observer. *Super Cam: Cam Newton's Rise to Panthers Greatness.* Chicago, IL: Triumph Books, 2016.

Doeden, Matt. *Football's Greatest Quarterbacks.* North Mankato, MN: Capstone Press, 2015.

Fishman, Jon M. *Cam Newton.* Minneapolis, MN: Lerner Publications, 2017.

Holmes, Parker. *Cam Newton.* New York, NY: PowerKids Press, 2013.

WEBSITES

Cam Newton Foundation
www.cam1newton.com/inside-cam
Read more about Cam on his foundation's official site.

Cam Newton Statistics
www.pro-football-reference.com/players/N/NewtCa00.htm
Find all of the latest stats.

Published in 2018 by Enslow Publishing, LLC
101 W. 23rd Street, Suite 240, New York, NY 10011

Copyright © 2018 by Enslow Publishing, LLC
All rights reserved.

No part of this book may be reproduced by any means without the written permission of the publisher.

Library of Congress Cataloging-in-Publication Data
Names: Shea, Therese, author.
Title: Cam Newton : MVP quarterback / Therese M. Shea.
Description: New York, NY : Enslow Publishing, [2018] | Series: Junior
  biographies | Includes bibliographical references and index.
Identifiers: LCCN 2016057577 | ISBN 9780766086647 (library bound : alk. paper) |ISBN 9780766087798 (pbk.)
  ISBN 9780766087804 (6-pack)
Subjects: LCSH: Newton, Cam, 1989- | Football players–United
  States–Biography. | Quarterbacks (Football)–United States–Biography.
Classification: LCC GV939.N42 S54 2017 | DDC 796.332092 [B] –dc23
LC record available at https://lccn.loc.gov/2016057577

Printed in the United States of America

To Our Readers: We have done our best to make sure all websites in this book were active and appropriate when we went to press. However, the author and the publisher have no control over and assume no liability for the material available on those websites or on any websites they may link to. Any comments or suggestions can be sent by email to customerservice@enslow.com.

Photo Credits: Cover, p. 1 Brian Killian/WireImage/Getty Images; p. 4 John Sciulli/WireImage/Getty Images; p. 6 John Salangsang/Invision/AP; p. 9 © Kenny Felt/ZUMA Press; p. 10 © Jim Dedmon/ZUMA Press.com; p. 11 Kelly Kline/Getty Images; p. 13 Rob Tringali/SportsChrome/Getty Images; p. 14 Sean Gardner/Getty Images; p. 16 Icon Sportswire/Getty Images; p. 19 Charlotte Observer/Tribune News Service/Getty Images; p. 20 Wesley Hitt/Getty Images; back cover, pp. 2, 3, 22, 23, 24 (curves graphic) Alena Kazlouskaya/Shutterstock.com; interior pages (gridiron) KeithBishop/DigitalVision Vectors/Getty Images.